Key Stage 2 Spelling Grammar and Punctuation

Author: Elizabeth Negus

© Copyright 2015 Elizabeth Negus

All rights reserved

This book shall not, by way of trade or otherwise, be lent, resold, hired out, or otherwise circulated without the prior consent of the copyright holder and the publisher in any form of binding or cover other than that in which it is published and without a similar condition including this condition being imposed on the subsequent purchaser. The use of its contents in any other media is also subject to the same conditions.

First Publication 2015

ISBN 978-1-910176-87-0

Second Publication 2017

ISBN 978-0-9956796-0-3

2017
Published by

Cerint Media
Essex
United Kingdom
www.cerintmedia.com

Contents

Sentences
Building Simple Sentences --- 7
Building Compound Sentences -- 8

Vocabulary
Improving your Vocabulary/Challenging Word ------------------------------- 10
Practice Building Sentences 1 -- 11
Confusing Words 1 -- 12
Practice Building Sentences 2 -- 13
Confusing Words 2 -- 14
Practice Building Sentences 3 -- 15

Prefixes and Suffixes
Understanding Prefixes and Suffixes --- 16
Using Prefixes and Suffixes --- 18

Parts of Speech
Using Adjectives --- 22
Using Adverbs -- 26
Types of Prepositions --- 28
Using Prepositions --- 31

Punctuation

The Comma --- 32
The Colon --- 32
The Semicolon --- 33
The Apostrophe --- 33
The Exclamation Mark --- 33
The Quotation Mark --- 34
Dash and The Hyphen --- 34
Ellipsis --- 35
The Full Stop/Period --- 35
Punctuation and Capitalisation --- 35
Punctuation- Using the Semicolon 1 --- 37
Punctuation - Using the Semicolon 2 --- 40

Grammar

Understanding the Rules of Grammar --- 42
Grammar exercises --- 44
Nouns --- 45
Pronouns --- 46

Language Techniques

Using Similes and Metaphors --- 47

Answers --- 50

Glossary --- 56

Introduction

Intellect is a key text book written to stretch and develop pupils reading and writing skills. The primary aim is always 'to make learning fun' whilst developing the pupil to a high competence level in literacy. This unique quality of fun learning and developing a mastermind for literacy is what makes Intellect outstanding.

Learning Strategies

Improve language skills in a structured context: grammar and vocabulary exercises teach students to avoid common mistakes. Intellect provides clear explanations and extensive practice of the grammar needed for Common Entrance and SATs exams..

Skills Practice

Immerse students in a wide range of topics to develop reading, writing, thinking, creative and imaginative skills.

Exam Practice

Familiarise students with the Common Entrance and SATs tests through authentic tasks: A variety of challenging, lively topics provide thorough training in exam skills and high level language development.

.

Answers

An answers appendix gives suggested answers for tasks where appropriate. Answer space for all questions is given in the workbook, the size of the space indicating the expected length of the response. A glossary of useful terms is also included for pupils development.

If you get some questions wrong, check your answers against the ones given on the answer sheet. Use your dictionary and / or work closely with your helper to learn and remember why the answer given is correct. When checking your comprehension question, the key is to re-read carefully both the passage and the question and carefully think it through.

Sentences

Building Simple Sentences

Each sentence below is missing a subject. Provide a suitable subject for each and write it in the space provided. Try to include descriptive words to suit the predicate meaning.

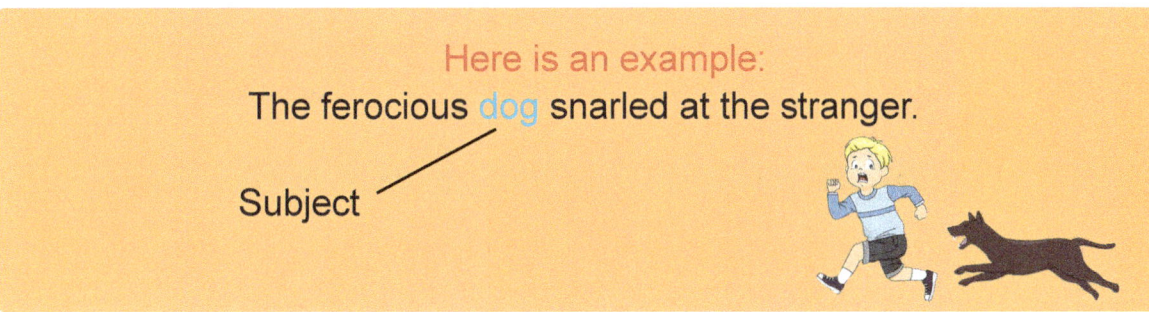

Here is an example:
The ferocious dog snarled at the stranger.

Subject

The word 'ferocious' helps explain why the dog (subject) snarled at the stranger.

1) _____ had rows of roses, daffodils and lilies.

2) _____ went to the theatre with their mum and dad.

3) _____ arrived in England for the second time.

4) _____ sailed across the ocean.

5) _____ prepared a delicious meal for Deirdre's birthday party.

6) _____ sang beautifully all night long.

7) _____ crawled under the bed.

8) _____ moved hastily through the crowded hall.

9) _____ hailed the cab driver.

10) _____ played the piano during the school concert.

Sentences

Building Compound Sentences

A compound sentence is made up of two simple sentences. Here are three examples of a compound sentence:

1. My cat was sleeping, so I went out to play.

2. I like vanilla  ice cream, but my friend likes chocolate.

3. The Thompson's wanted to go to Italy, because they wanted to see Venice.

Write five compound sentences to show that you understand its meanings.

1) _____

_____

2) _____

_____

Sentences

Practice Building Compound Sentences

3) _____

   _____

4) _____

   _____

5) _____

   _____

6) In the space provided explain the importance of using compound sentences in your writing.

_____
_____
_____

Vocabulary

Improving your Vocabulary

To improve your descriptive vocabulary, look up the meaning of the following adjectives in your dictionary and record the words and definitions in your personal notebook. Then use each word in a sentence of your own to show you understand what it means.

Challenging Vocabulary

Enthusiastic	Evasive
Cluttered	Ambitious
Cloudy	Amused
Clumsy	Amazing
Colossal	Excellent
Coherent	Angry
Comfortable	Ancient
Complex	Annoyed
Condemned	Anxious
Conscious	Attractive
Courageous	Magnificent
Erratic	Atrocious
Envious	Happy

Vocabulary

Practice Building Sentences 1

Choose 10 of your favourite words from the above list to form sentences of your own.

1) _____

2) _____

3) _____

4) _____

5) _____

6) _____

7) _____

8) _____

9) _____

10) _____

Vocabulary

Confusing Words 1

Below are a set of words that are often confused because they look alike or sound similar. Circle the words that match the meaning.

1.	Accept/except	To receive
2.	Already/all ready	Before or by the time set
3.	Altogether/all together	Wholly or thoroughly
4.	Among/between	Use among with objects of three or more(group)
5.	Anyone/any one	Any person at all
6.	Further/farther	Geographical distance
7.	Lie/lay	To put or place something down
8.	It's/its	A contraction of it is
9.	Maybe/may be	One is a verb
10.	Principle/principal	Chief; main person
11.	Raise/rise	To lift or cause to move upwards
12.	There/their	Possessive form of they

Vocabulary

Practice Building Sentences 2

Use the following words to make sentences to show their meaning.

1) whose _____
   _____

2) reason _____
   _____

3) myself _____
   _____

4) everyone _____
   _____

5) sight _____
   _____

Vocabulary

Confusing Words 2

Match each of the words in column A to their correct definitions in column B

COLUMN A	COLUMN B
Immense	Pay attention to
Moral	Understand
Elaborate	Tiredness
Diligent	Check out
Banish	Huge
Deface	Hard working
Heed	Expand on
Fatigue	Honest
Inspect	Send away
Deduce	Damage

Vocabulary

Practice Building Sentences 3

Choose five words from Column A and use them in a sentence of your own to show that you understand their meaning.

1) _____

2) _____

3) _____

4) _____

5) _____

Choose five words from Column B and use them in a sentence of your own to show that you understand their meaning.

1) _____

2) _____

3) _____

4) _____

5) _____

Prefixes and Suffixes

Understanding prefixes and suffixes

A prefix is a word part that is added to the front of a base word to change the meaning of that word. More than one prefix may mean the same thing.

Examples: The prefixes dis-, mis-, and un- mean "not," or "the opposite of"

dis + approve = disapprove (not approve)
mis + inform = misinform (not inform)
un + happy = unhappy (not happy)

A suffix is a word part that is added to the end of a base word. A suffix usually changes the meaning of the word.

Examples:

Pass + able = passable (able to pass)
move + ment = movement (the act of moving)
kind + ness = kindness (being kind)

The suffix -able means "able to be"
The suffix -ment means "the act of"
The suffix -ness means "being"

Prefixes and Suffixes

Practice Question

Use the correct prefix and suffix in front of each word

Word	Prefix	Suffix
Pleasant		
Appoint		
Fortune		
Believe		
Respect		
Enjoy		
Regard		
Behave		
Agree		
Finished		
Able		
Skilled		
Deserved		
Happy		

Prefixes and Suffixes

Using prefixes and suffixes

Circle the correct **prefix** to go with each base word. Then use the new word in a sentence.

1) satisfied un-, dis-, re-

   _____

2) direct un-, dis-, re-

   _____

3) cover un-, tri-, bi-

   _____

4) communicate dis-, post-, ex-

   _____

5) obey ex-, tri-, dis-

   _____

6) hale dis-, ex-, un-

   _____

Prefixes and Suffixes

Using prefixes and suffixes

Circle the correct suffix to go with each base word. Then use the new word in a sentence.

1) depart -able, -ment, -ly

   _____

2) happy -able, -ment, -ness

   _____

3) manage -able, -ly, -ness

   _____

4) respect -able, -ful, -ness

   _____

5) laugh -ing, -ment, -ness

   _____

6) arrange -able, -ment, -ness

   _____

Prefixes and Suffixes

Practice Building Sentences

Using your dictionary list ten other prefixes of your choice. Please provide their meaning.

Prefix	Meaning

Prefixes and Suffixes

Practice Building Sentences

Using your dictionary list ten other suffixes of your choice. Please provide their meaning.

Suffix	Meaning

Parts of Speech

Using Adjectives

We use adjectives to describe nouns. Carefully read the passage and underline all the adjectives in the passage.

Imagine waking up to the lovely sounds of chirping birds outside your window. It is springtime and all the birds are singing. You crawl out of your comfortable bed and peep through the glass to see a delicate nest in the tree top. The nest is made from things like dried grass, twigs, moss, feathers or animal hair. You tip-toe closer to the window and there you spot a red-breast robin nestling with her beautiful chicks.

The birds are unaware that they are being watched. The mother flies in and out of the nest carrying food for her babies. The babies look helpless every time they crane their little necks to eat the food. Their wings are not fully developed and this makes it difficult for them to fly.

Parts of Speech

Using Adjectives

The mother is extremely protective over her babies. She is always on the lookout for predators. She perches herself and tilts her head swiftly from side to side every time she senses the slightest noise.

Practice Question

Use the Adjectives you have underlined in sentences of your own to show you understand their meaning:

1) _____

2) _____

3) _____

4) _____

5) _____

6) _____

Parts of Speech

Using Adjectives

Adjectives describe things. Here are some Examples:

A stormy day!

Adjectives

Sade is wearing an elegant dress.

Practice Question

Listed below are five adjectives. Use them in a sentence of your own to show that you understand their meaning.

| diligent | gifted | caring |
| outstanding | cheerful | |

1) _____

2) _____

3) _____

4) _____

5) _____

Parts of Speech

Using Adjectives

Look at the underlined words in the following sentences and think of more unusual adjectives that could replace them.

1) What a <u>nice</u> dress you are wearing!

   _____

2) The food is <u>tasty</u>.

   _____

3) I like reading <u>good</u> books.

   _____

4) The soldier's behaviour was <u>awful</u>!

   _____

5) We had <u>bad</u> weather in Spain.

   _____

Parts of Speech

Using Adverbs

An adverb modifies the verb. It tells you how something is done. It often ends in - /y Here are some Examples:

The child was breathing (heavily).   James ran (quickly).

Adverb

Practice Question

Read the passage below and circle all the verbs and underline the adverbs.

Happily, Sophie ran out of the house to greet her mum and dad who had been away on holiday. They were all very excited to see each other. Sophie's dad gently hugged her while her mum looked excitedly at how beautiful she looked. The three got into the car and mum drove slowly and carefully through the country lanes. It was a bright sunny day; it reminded Sophie's parents of their holiday in the tropical island of St. Lucia. The fields were covered with brightly coloured yellow daffodils and the trees swayed lightly in the warm breeze. At midday, mum, dad and Sophie arrived at their country cottage. They walked slowly along the garden path leading to the front door. Sophie peeped through the window, "Hello! Is anybody home?" she whispered softly. Boobers, the family cat, leapt through the window, and landed on all fours in Sophie's arms. "You're the best," said Sophie, cheerfully!

Parts of Speech

Using Adverbs

Complete the table below with your own examples of verbs and adverbs:

Verbs	Adverbs

Parts of Speech

Types of Prepositions

Prepositions: A preposition is a word that indicates where something is.

Here are three examples below:

a.   The cat is in the basket.

b.   The dog is under the table.

c.   The cup is on the table.

In, under and on are all prepositions. They are showing where the cat, dog and cup are. Prepositions can also show location in time.

Read the next three examples:

1.   At midday, Tom left the school.

2.   In the spring, the birds sing.

3.   During the race, Jack stopped to have a drink of water.

Parts of Speech

Types of Prepositions

Below is a full list of prepositions to study and learn.

Prepositions- Study and Learn

About	Around	On
Above	As	Up
According to	As for	Upon
Across	At	Up to
After	Because of	With
Against	on top of	Within
Like	Out	Without
Near	Out of	But*
Next	Outside	By
Of	Over	By means of
Along	Past	Before
Along with	Regarding	Behind
Among	Off	Below
Apart from	Up	Beneath

Parts of Speech

Types of Prepositions

Prepositions- Study and Learn

Beside	In back of	In place of
Between	In case of	Inside
Because of	Concerning	In spite of
Beyond	Despite	Instead of
During	Down	Into
Except	Through	
Except for	Throughout	
Excepting	Till	
For	To	
From	Toward	
Onto	Under	
Since	Underneath	
In	Unlike	
In addition to	In front of	

* But is sometimes used as a preposition to mean "except". For example, Everyone but Janet had ice cream.

Parts of Speech

Using Prepositions

Circle the prepositions in the following sentences.

1. The box is beneath the car.
2. Underneath the window pane is a slug.
3. In front of the house is a bed of roses.
4. The pen is on the table.
5. Roger put the milk in the fridge.
6. The computer is next to the desk.
7. Everyone likes cake but Sam.
8. The crow flew over the trees.
9. Jane is sitting on the fence.
10. There are two houses between the supermarket and the cinema.

Punctuation

The Comma (,)

The comma is used to show a separation of ideas or elements within the structure of a sentence. Additionally, it is used in numbers, dates and letter writing after the salutation and closing.

- **Direct address:** This was very kind of you, Sir David Negus.
- **Separation of two complete sentences:** Michael and Deirdre went to the museum, and afterwards treated themselves to afternoon tea at Harrods.
- **Separating lists or elements within sentences:** Perry bought a black Armani suit, a black belt, two pairs of shoes and a brief case.

The Colon (:)

A colon (:) has three main uses. The first is after a word introducing a quotation, an explanation, an example, or a series.

- Richie was planning to study four subjects at university: English, Law, German and Politics.

The second is between independent clauses, when the second explains the first, similar to a semicolon:

- Mother did not have time to change into her evening gown: She was already late from the Press Conference.

The third use of a colon is for emphasis:

- Having carefully observed Jason, there was one thing he loved more than any other: his violin!

A colon also has non-grammatical uses in time, ratio, business correspondence and references.

Punctuation

The Semicolon (;)

The semicolon (;) is used to connect independent clauses. It shows a closer relationship between the clauses than a full stop would show.

- Ranita was very excited; she knew she had won the Letter-Writing competition and would be lunching at the House of Lords.

The Apostrophe (')

An apostrophe (') is used to indicate the omission of a letter or letters from a word, the possessive case, or the plurals of lowercase letters.

Examples of the apostrophe in use include:
- **Omission of letters from a word:** I've read the Lord of the Rings countless times. I wasn't the only one who found the book captivating.
- **Possessive case:** Mark's bird flew away.
- **Plural for lowercase letters:** Seven school children were told to mind their p's and q's.

The Exclamation Mark (!)

1. To show emotion/feelings

Punctuation

The Quotation Mark(" ")

Quotation marks (" ") are a pair of punctuation marks used primarily to mark the beginning and end of a passage attributed to another and repeated word for word. They are also used to indicate meanings and to indicate the unusual status of a word.
- "Stop climbing over the neighbour's fence," she shouted.

Single quotation marks (') are used most frequently for quotes within quotes.
- Mr George told the teacher, "I saw Marc in the Chemistry lab, and he said to me 'Sarah started the experiment ahead of the exams,' and I believed him."

Dash (---) and the Hyphen (-)

Two other common punctuation marks are the dash and hyphen. These marks are often confused with each other due to their appearance but they are very different.

A hyphen is used to join two or more words together into a compound term and is not separated by spaces. For example, mother-in-law, full-time.

A dash is used to separate words into statements. There are two common types of dashes: en dash and em dash.
- **En dash:** Slightly wider than a hyphen, the en dash is a symbol (–) that is used in writing or printing to indicate a range or connections and differentiations, such as 2010–2017 or London–Edinburgh trains.
- **Em dash:** Twice as long as the en dash, the em dash can be used in place of a comma, parenthesis, or colon to enhance readability or emphasise the conclusion of a sentence. For example, Mrs Donnegon was angry and gave a direct reply — No!

Punctuation

Ellipsis (. . .)

The ellipsis is most commonly represented by three periods (. . .) although it is occasionally demonstrated with three asterisks (***). The ellipsis is used in writing or printing to indicate an omission, especially of letters or words. Ellipses are frequently used within quotations to jump from one phrase to another, omitting unnecessary words that do not interfere with the meaning. Students writing research papers or newspapers quoting parts of speeches will often employ ellipsis to avoid copying lengthy text that is not needed.

- Omission of words: James commenced the countdown, "Ten, nine, eight, seven …" until he got to 0, then galloped off to find Harry.

The Full Stop/Period (.)

1. To show possession for nouns and indefinite pronouns
2. To contract/shorten words

Punctuation and Capitalisation

Read the following passage adding the correct punctuation marks where they belong.

some of my friends waste their money on computer games while i do things that are more interesting and make me happy do you want to know what i do i collect the stamps from old letters and place them in my gibbons stamp album collecting stamps is a great way of learning about other countries i study the history of the country i also make money from it because the value of my stamps keeps increasing do you collect stamps someone who collects stamps is called a philatelist in my stamp album i have stamps from the caribbean asia and africa try it you might like it

Punctuation

Punctuation and Capitalisation

i started collecting stamps when i was fifteen years old i needed a fascinating hobby to distract me from some of the things that happened at my school at aged 13 my parents enrolled me at princeton boys boarding school there were approximately 2000 pupils some of them join in the sixth form and continue right through until they are 18 although princeton provided many sporting opportunities to learn and develop my love for history and holitics drew me closer to my stamp collection I dream of becoming a professional philatelist one day

my best friend was thomas and he was an avid stamp collector every summer after fishing we would go to the shopping centres the library the car boot sales and museums to either buy old stamps or learn something more about stamps around the world this summer my parents have decided to go camping in the scottish highlands i can't wait to sit in front a camp fire gazing at my parents eating haggis while i indulge in licking stamps

Punctuation

Punctuation and Semicolon 1

The semicolon- the semicolon connects closely related independent clauses.

Example: Edwyna sang beautifully; the orchestra played her favourite songs.

Notice that the topic is Edwyna and the way she sings, and the clause following the semicolon adds information or supports the idea of the clause that goes before it.

Match each independent clause from Column A with a related one from Column B.

COLUMN A	COLUMN B
Some bread rolls are crusty	her lessons are always fun and exciting.
The holiday to Scotland was planned for Sunday	my favourite places are Barbados, Israel and Bali.
Miss Thompson is an excellent teacher	the police said they would look for it.
The thief stole a valuable painting from the museum	I packed my suitcase the night before.
I like hot countries	fortunately, it was only a drill.
The fire alarm sounded in the school's hall	however, others are not.

Punctuation

Punctuation and Semicolon 1

I attend the fashion shows	I still need to put tiles on the floor.
My pet hamster is called Joey	they have known each other for ten years.
I have painted the house	my brother goes to the pop clubs.
Peter and John went to the same school	he likes eating carrots .

Write the *independent clauses* connected by a *semicolon* in the spaces provided.

a) Some bread rolls are crusty _____

_____

b) The holiday to Scotland was planned for Sunday _____

_____

c) Miss Thompson is an excellent teacher _____

_____

Punctuation

Punctuation and Semicolon 1

Write the independent clauses connected by a semicolon in the spaces provided.

d) The thief stole a valuable painting from the museum _____

_____

e) I like hot countries _____

_____

f) The fire alarm sounded in the school's hall _____

_____

g) I attend the fashion shows _____

_____

h) My pet hamster is called Joey _____

_____

Punctuation

Punctuation and Semicolon 1

Write the independent clauses connected by a semicolon in the spaces provided.

i) I have painted the house _____

_____

j) Peter and John went to the same school _____

_____

Punctuation and Semicolon 2

Put a tick next to the sentences where semicolons have been used correctly.

1. He liked the new building; she did not. ☐

2. Anna told me her birthday wish; she would like a new mobile phone. ☐

3. The cat is sitting on; the window pane. ☐

4. I bought a bouquet of red roses; last weekend. ☐

5. Scotland is a beautiful place; you should visit there one day. ☐

Punctuation

Punctuation and Semicolon 2

Put a tick next to the sentences where semicolons have been used correctly.

6. Malcolm plays golf every month; he now teaches Jack how to play. ☐

7. The shop is close; to the library. ☐

8. Sam would like to go; to the book festival this year. ☐

Rewrite these sentences, and replace the conjunction with a semicolon.

1) The cottage was open but there was no one inside to welcome me.

_____

2) The plane journey from England to Australia is long so I bought two books to read.

_____

3) Margaret wants to study French whereas Hannah wants to study Latin

_____

4) The Caribbean countries are hilly but many European countries are flat.

_____

Grammar

Understanding the Rules of Grammar

Noun Plurals

Here are five basic rules for making nouns plurals; however, there are many exceptions to these rules.

Rule 1

Most nouns form the plural by adding s to the singular nouns.

Examples: stone – stones   chocolate – chocolates
            Pen – pens   window – windows

Rule 2

Nouns ending in "f" or "fe"
In some cases add s to the original nouns

Examples: cliff – cliffs   chief – chiefs

Nouns ending in "fe" changes to v and add "es"
Examples: Life – lives   Knife – knives

Rule 3

Nouns ending in s or sh, eh, x and z
Add es to the singular noun

Example: Business – Businesses

Bus – buses   Bunch – bunches   Box – boxes
Rush – rushes   Hex – hexes   Buzz – buzzes

Grammar

Understanding the Rules of Grammar

Rule 4

There are times when the noun ends in f and s has to be added to make it plural.

Example: roof – roofs

If the singular noun ends in -y, change the ending to -ies.

Example: City – Cities   Puppy – Puppies

If the singular noun ends in -o, add -es to make it plural.

Example: Potato – Potatoes   Tomato – Tomatoes

Rule 5

If a vowel comes before the o ending, in most cases add s

Radio – Radios   Video – Videos

If a consonant comes before the o ending, in most cases add 'es'
Example: Solo – Solos   Piano – Pianos

Note: Irregular nouns should be checked in the dictionary because they follow no specific rules.

Example: Child-Children   Goose-Geese   Man- Men

Some nouns don't change at all when they're pluralised.

Example: Sheep – Sheep   Moose – Moose   Deer – Deer

Grammar

Grammar Exercise

Usually, when a word ends in 'f' or 'fe' we change the 'f' to 'V' and add 'es' or 's' to make it plural. Numbers 1 and 2 have been done for you. Complete the rest of the chart.

1. Loaf — Loaves

2. Calf — Calves

3. Half — _____

4. Knife — _____

5. Life — _____

6. Thief — _____

7. Wife — _____

8. Leaf — _____

9. Self — _____

10. Wolf — _____

Grammar

Nouns

A noun is a word that represents a person, place or thing.

Example of proper nouns: Elizabeth, Princess, David, Joshua

Example of common nouns: flower, rocks, pencil, chocolate

Example of collective nouns: a bouquet of flowers, a herd of cattle, a flock of birds, a pride of lions.

Underline the word in each list that is not a noun.

1. Michael, carpet, cars, yell
2. England, Venice, sleepy, river
3. Avenue, phone, villa, see
4. Find, board, teacher, computer
5. Celia, John, Perry, run
6. Biscuits, television, juice, delicious
7. Jewellery, whisper, shoes, coats
8. Travel, airport, suitcase, screen
9. Tree, cookies, sing, bells
10. Moon, galaxy, hear, sun

Grammar

Pronouns

A pronoun takes the place of a noun. Here are some examples of pronouns: I, me, he, she, herself, you, it, someone, everybody, their.

Sentence: Fred likes football. He plays for Manchester United.

The pronoun he takes the place of Fred.

Circle the pronouns in the following sentences:

1. Jack and Jill went up the hill. They both fell down.

2. Deborah likes running. She goes to the gym every week.

3. Do you think he won the prize?

4. Look! Someone is picking the apples from Mr. Smith's garden.

5. Do you have any more cherries to share?

6. I am going to the party and it will be great fun!

7. Gina and Carol smiled when they recognised their father.

8. Everybody is afraid of something.

9. Do you want to tell me about your new school?

10. She smiled to herself at getting top marks in English.

Language Techniques

Using Similes and Metaphors

What is a simile?
A simile is a comparison between two unlike things using the words *like* or *as*.
Example: She walked *like* a chicken.

What is a metaphor?
A metaphor is a comparison between two things without using the words like, as, or as if.
Example: She is an angel.

Tick the appropriate boxes for the similes and metaphors.

	Similes	Metaphors
The snow is a white blanket.	☐	☐
I slept like a baby.	☐	☐
The world is a stage.	☐	☐
John is a shining star.	☐	☐
She is a peacock.	☐	☐
You sing as sweet as a nightingale.	☐	☐
It is raining cats and dogs!	☐	☐
The rain dropped like bullets on the roof.	☐	☐
The snow formed a white blanket on the ground.	☐	☐
I imagined my legs were tree trunks.	☐	☐

Language Techniques

Using Similes and Metaphors

Read the following paragraph. Find the simile or metaphor and underline it.

This morning we went camping in the Scottish Highlands. The sun was a ball of fire when the chief scout woke us up. I was as hungry as a bear and was looking forward to breakfast. Every morning the leader would wake us up at the crack of dawn for breakfast. The breakfast was always eggs, bacon and sausages. Sometimes the scrambled eggs were piled as high as mountains on my plate. After eating, I always felt like a beached whale!

Give six similes and six metaphors of your own and write them in the boxes provided below.

SIMILES

1)

2)

3)

4)

5)

6)

Language Techniques

Using Similes and Metaphors

METAPHORS

1)
2)
3)
4)
5)
6)

Answers

Sentences

Page 7

Here are examples of usage of the words provided. Answers may vary:

1. The beautiful garden had rows of roses, daffodils and lilies.
2. The excited children went to the theatre with their mum and dad.
3. The exhausted mountain climbers arrived in England for the second time.
4. The historic Titanic once sailed the ocean.
5. The excellent chef prepared a delicious meal for Mary's birthday party.
6. St. Paul's classical choir sang beautifully all night long.
7. The frightened dog crawled under the bed.
8. The anxious policeman moved hastily through the crowded hall.
9. The terrified gentleman hailed the cab driver.
10. James skilfully played the piano during the school concert.

Pages 8-9

Here are 10 examples of compound sentences. Answers may vary.

1. Mark ran down the street and his parents waved from the house.
2. The dog came rushing in so the cat jumped in the hedge.
3. My friend gave me an umbrella because it was raining.
4. I like apples and oranges
5. Joe did not take on the test because he was away on holiday.
6. I think I will buy aunt's car and sell the blue one.
7. I really want to go to the theatre, but I am too tired to drive.
8. I am on a diet, yet I really want the chocolate pudding.
9. The teachers got there early, and they got really good seats.
10. There was no ice cream at home, nor did we have money to go to the supermarket.

Vocabulary

Page 11

Your sentences should be like this.

1. Andy Murray is very enthusiastic about playing tennis.
2. What a magnificent portrait of the Sistine Chapel!
3. In the sixteenth century men and women were condemned to prison for speaking against the monarchy.
4. Jack lost his way because he thought that the directions to the office building were too complex.
5. Mandy's attendance over the last term was rather erratic.
6. Jack's friends considered him to be very courageous for climbing Mount Everest.
7. Father was annoyed with the plumber for cancelling the afternoon appointment.

Answers

8. Mrs Jones, the school's matron, complained about the boys' room being cluttered with junk!

9. The armchair is extremely comfortable to sit in.

10. "This game is more complex than I thought," he admitted.

Page 12

You should have circled;

1. Accept
2. Already
3. Altogether
4. Among
5. Anyone
6. Farther
7. Lie
8. It's
9. May be
10. Principal
11. Raise
12. Their

Page 13

Your sentences should look like this.

1. Whose mobile phone keeps ringing?

2. For some reason Christine had always thought Abby would adjust quickly to her new school.

3. I can see myself in the mirror.

4. After everyone left the concert, Celia and John went to speak to the director.

5. The sight of rotten eggs made her stomach roll again.

Page 14

You should have matched:

Immense → Huge
Moral → Honest
Elaborate → Expand on
Diligent → Hard working
Banish → Send away
Deface → Damage
Heed → Pay attention to
Fatigue → Tired
Inspect → Check out
Deduce → Work out or derive

Page 15

Your Sentences should look like this:

1. It is important to elaborate on your exam answers.

2. The commander will inspect the boots on Friday.

3. Pedestrians should always take heed of the road safety instructions.

4. There is immense pressure on school children to perform well in all subjects.

5. The king promises to banish anyone who behaves unruly in his presence.

Answers

Prefixes and Suffixes

Page 17

You should have written these in Prefix:

Unpleasant, Disappoint, Insincere, Disbelieve, Disrespect, Disregard, Misbehave, Disagree and Unable

You should have written these in Suffix:

Enjoyable, Agreeable, Endless, Government, Beautifully, Happily, Argument and Boldness in Suffix.

Page 18

For prefixes, you should have circled;

1. dis: I was dissatisfied with the food menu.
2. re: The traffic was redirected due to the motorway.
3. un: The pirates uncovered a gold chest containing.
4. un: Kindly untie the ribbons on the red box.
5. dis: Children are put on detention when they disobey.
6. ex: The doctor suggested that the runners should exhale slowly over three seconds and repeat until calm.

Page 19

For suffixes, you should have circled;

1. ment: The shoe department at Selfridges offers a wide range of boots.
2. ness: Bubbling with happiness, Deirdre hummed her favourite song as she skipped down the corridors.
3. able: Jane finds spending three hours in the gym is manageable after her French lessons.
4. ness: The skiers can approach no nearer because of the hardness of the snow, which is very firmly packed.
5. ing: Stephen could not stop laughing at the clown.
6. ment: I made an arrangement to meet with the netball team on Wednesday.

Parts of Speech

Pages 22-23

You should have underlined the following Adjectives in the passage:

1. Lovely
2. Comfortable
3. Delicate
4. Beautiful
5. Helpless
6. Little

Page 24

You should have written sentences like this:

1. diligent - Mrs Charles, the English teacher, believes the diligent students will check their answers.
2. gifted -The school has recognised Jason as a gifted and talented boy.
3. caring - Jane is a caring person who puts the needs of others first.
4. outstanding -This academic year, the pupils produced outstanding results in English.
5. cheerful -It's not difficult to find," he said, with a cheerful smile.

Answers

Page 25
Replacing with unusual adjective

1. What an elegant dress you are wearing.
2. The food is sumptuous.
3. I like reading educational books.
4. The soldier's behaviour was despicable!
5. We had inclement weather in Spain.

Page 26
For verbs, you should have circled;
ran, greet, stared, drove, reminded, swayed, arrived, walked, peeped and whispered

For adverbs, you should have underlined; happily, excitedly, slowly, carefully, brightly, lightly, softly and cheerfully.

Page 31
For the preposition, you should have circled;

1. beneath
2. underneath
3. in front
4. on
5. in
6. next to
7. but
8. over
9. between

Punctuation

Pages 35-36 Punctuation and Capitalisation
The following passage shows the correct punctuation marks where they belong.

Some of my friends waste their money on computer games while I do things that are more interesting and make me happy. Do you want to know what I do? I collect the stamps from old letters and place them in my Gibbons stamp album. Collecting stamps is a great way of learning about other countries. I study the history of the country; I also make money from it because the value of my stamps keeps increasing. Do you collect stamps? Someone who collects stamps is called a philatelist. In my stamp album I have stamps from the Caribbean, Asia and Africa. Try it you might like it!

I started collecting stamps when I was fifteen years old. I needed a fascinating hobby to distract me from some of the things that happened at my school. There were about seventy boys and girls in my school year and they went from four to sixteen years of age. My best friend was Thomas and he was an avid stamp collector. Every summer after fishing, we would go to the shopping centres, the library, the car boot sales and museums to either buy old stamps or learn something more about stamps around the world. This summer, my parents have decided to go camping in the Scottish Highlands. I can't wait to sit in front a camp fire, gazing at my parents eating haggis, while I indulge in sticking on stamps!

Answers

Punctuation

Pages 37-40

The independent clauses below show the correct connection using the semicolon.

a. Some bread rolls are crusty; however, others are not.

b. The holiday to Scotland was planned for Sunday; I packed my suitcase the night before.

c. Miss Thompson is an excellent teacher; her lessons are always fun and exciting.

d. The thief stole a valuable painting from the museum; the police said they would look for it.

e. I like hot countries; my favourite places are Barbados, Israel and Bali.

f. The fire alarm sounded in the school's hall; fortunately, it was only a drill.

g. I attend the fashion shows; my brother goes to the pop clubs.

h. My pet hamster is called Joey; he likes eating carrots.

i. I have painted the house; I still need to put tiles on the floor.

j. Peter and John went to the same school; they have known each other for ten years.

Pages 40-41

You should have ticked nos. 1,2,5 and 6;

1. He liked the new building; she did not.
2. Anna told me her birthday wish; she would like a new mobile phone.
5. Scotland is a beautiful place; you should visit there one day.
6. Malcolm plays golf every month; he now teaches Jack how to play.

Page 41

Corrected sentences where the conjunction has been replaced with a semicolon are:

1. The cottage was open; there was no one inside to welcome me.
2. The plane journey from England to Australia is long; I bought two adventure books to read.
3. Margaret wants to study French; Hannah wants to study Latin.
4. The Caribbean countries are hilly; many European countries are flat.

Grammar

Page 44 Changing 'f' to 'v' and adding 'es' or 's'.

1. Loaf → Loaves
2. Calf → Calves
3. Half → halves
4. Knife → knives
5. Life → lives
6. Thief → thieves
7. Wife → wives
8. Leaf → leaves
9. Self → selves
10. Wolf → wolves

Answers

Page 45 Nouns

You should have underlined:

1. yell
2. sleepy
3. see
4. find
5. run
6. delicious
7. whisper
8. travel
9. sing
10. hear

Page 46 Pronouns

You should have circled:

1. They
2. She
3. He
4. Someone
5. You
6. It
7. They
8. Everybody
9. You
10. She

Similes and Metaphors

Page 47

For Similes, you should have ticked the box with the below sentences:

I slept like a baby.
You sing as sweet as a nightingale.
The rain dropped like bullets on the roof.

Page 47

For Metaphors, you should have ticked the box with the below sentences:

The snow is a white blanket.
The world is a stage.
John is a shining star.
She is a peacock.
It is raining cats and dogs!
The snow formed a white blanket on the ground.
I imagined my legs were tree trunks.

Page 48

For Simile, you should have underlined:

As hungry as a bear (Simile)
As high as mountains (Simile)
Like a beached whale! (Simile)

Page 48

For Metaphor, you should have underlined:

A ball of fire (Metaphor)
Crack of dawn (Metaphor)

For Similes, you should have written sentences similar to these;

a. The dog ate his food like a vacuum cleaner.

b. Emmanuel's arms were weak and felt like chicken noodles.

c. The children's cheers were as loud as fireworks.

d. Mark slept like a baby.

e. After the competition, Sarah was as sweet as pie.

f. Joshua is like a computer when he does his mat.

Answers

Page 49

For Metaphors, you should have written sentences similar to these;

a. Catherine was a beacon of sunshine when she gave her triumph speech.
b. The cat's fur was a blanket of warmth.
c. The inside of the log cabin was a refrigerator.
d. Bobby's car was a fighter jet when he drove passed us.
e. The plane roared through the sky.
f. The crockery danced on the table during the earthquake.

Glossary of Terms

This glossary presents brief explanations of terms often used in English language.

Pronoun - The pronoun takes the place of a noun. Perry is playing badminton and he is winning.

Semicolon - The semicolon joins two closely related clauses in a sentence.

Sentence - A set of words which form a grammatically complete statement, usually containing a subject, verb, and object. The flowers are on the table.

Simile - A figure of speech in which one thing is directly likened to another by using the word as or like. Your face glows like the morning sun.

Suffix - The ending part of a word that changes the meaning of the word. Thank-ful, harm-less, wash-able.

Vocabulary - The particular selection or types of words chosen in speech or writing.

Glossary of Terms

Adjective - The part of speech modifying the noun or pronoun: a red dress.

Adverb - The part of speech modifying a verb, an adjective or another adverb: quickly moving.

Colon - The colon introduces a list of things: rice, milk, break, cake, sugar, oil.

Comma - The comma separates items in a sentence: I like apples, plums, mangoes and grapes. The comma also separates phrases and some clauses.

Comprehension - The ability to understand something.

Exclamation mark - The exclamation mark shows feeling: Help!

Question mark - A punctuation symbol "?" written at the end of a sentence to indicate a direct question. How old are you?

Full stop/Period - A punctuation mark indicating the end of a sentence. The room is crowded.

Grammar - The study of sentence structure, especially with the use of correct sentences and correct vocabulary. I spoke to my teacher, Mr. Bright.

Metaphor - A figure of speech in which one thing is described in terms of another. Christine is a ray of sunshine.

Noun - A noun is the name given to a person, place or thing: ribbon, train, grass, flowers and shoe.

Parts of speech - The eight common parts of speech are the verb, noun, adjective, adverb, pronoun, preposition, conjunction, and interjection.

Prefix - A prefix is placed at the beginning of a word to change its meaning. Pre means "before." Prefixes may also indicate a location, number, or time. Root: central part of a word. dis-like, re-move, un-kind.

Preposition - A word which tells you where one thing is in relation to another. The mouse is under the table.